A YEAR

ON THE BUS

poet on a bus

Cover, illustrations and pictures by Stefan Wirth
Words by Stefan Wirth
Biography by Janni Nielsen
Editing by Janni Nielsen
Special thanks to Vanessa Hanni

Production and Publishing: BoD – Books on Demand, Norderstedt
ISBN: 978-3-75620-078-8

Stefan Wirth a.k.a. "poet on a bus" resides and works in Innbruck. He firmly believes that words can change a place and tries to do so by carrying poetry into urban spaces. Besides writing, the theoretical architect likes to kick back creating visual projects and finds balance on the Lacrosse pitch.

Stefan has a dislike for thoughtless and rash words as well as bad coffee. He dreams of portraying a serial killer on stage and of working with horses in Canada one day.

CONTENTS

SPRING

And here I am, again... Four in the morning, on my way home from a party I really didn't want to attend. Or if I did, at least I didn't want to drink. Well, that didn't work out too well, again, didn't it. And so I stumble home again through the bittersweet twilight. You know what I mean, that thin red line when you still ride the wave of euphoria, but the looming hangover you already know will hit you like a sledgehammer and make you regret everything that brought you to this point, is only moments away. If I get to bed fast enough, everything will be fine –otherwise it will be bad, very bad.

The Serles is already touched by the first beams of sunlight and you can hear the birds. Oh, how I hate those reproachful chirps that tell you how you overdid it again, tonight. Music is my last resort against that birdsong, so put the headphones on and turn the music up loud. Connor Oberst finally drowns out the chirping birds. He sings about Mamah Borthwick and Frank Lloyd Wright. Huh, Frank Lloyd Wright.... He has always been my favorite architect. With him, genius and madness always seemed to be very close together, but that seems to be normal with architects. Why I know this, you ask? From my own experience of course. Madness is slowly taking me over too – and with it comes fear...

The most beautiful thing about you?
You are...
What else could anyone need...?

She hoped, I'm forever cursed
but you bring out the best in me
when I'm feeling worst...

To arms! To arms!
Get up my friends!
Abandon your guns,
get to your pens!

Arm your kids with education,
love & passion,
dedication.

Arm yourself with empathy,
with kindness,
basic human decency.

To arms! To arms!
Be gentle though.
What's sown today,
tomorrow might grow...

So, tell me..., she says,
why are you doing this?

> Doing what, I asked.

Well, the writing, she inquires.

> Hmmm.... Why do you breath, I ask.

What kind of question is that?
I have to breathe to survive, she says.

> So, there's your answer...,
> I reply, and drink up.

To be or not to be?
I hate to be
indifferent!

Hey, I wrote you a poem,
I hope you don't mind.
But that's what we do,
we drink and we write.

I just hope that you're happy
'cause I ain't seen you in years
I don't know what happened,
you just disappeared.

I guess our lifes changed,
I know, yours more than mine.
I'm just missing your soul,
and our coffees with wine.

Oh, I hate all this silence
but I'll wait 'til I'm sore.
If you still need some time,
I'll just wait some more...

I'm embracing the night,
for the moonlight
is a poet's sunshine...

What else is a poet
but a foolish drunkard
who happens to be good with words...?

I could do that!

Yes, you could do it.
But you didn't!

I'd walk through the desert
I'd swim through the sea.
I'd climb all the mountains.
And then I'd repeat.
I'd kill all your demons
if it'd make you see,
I adore you,
love you,
I won't let you be...

I write about feelings
not people.
'Cause feelings is all I know...

I try everyday just to tell you
I think of you a little bit more.
I'm hoping today I won't miss you
But I will do for sure.

I try everyday just to tell you
I fell for you a little bit more.
I can't find the words to begin with.
My heart and mind are at war.

I'm just too afraid to tell you.
A foolish excuse, oh I know.
But I'm afraid you'd be leaving
from the moment you know...

All you did was
making me feel...

There might come a day
I won't remember you.
Yet I will always
remember that feeling...

You are like
a submarine in my mind
surfacing at the strangest of times...

You're sorry you're tired,
I'm sorry you care.
I'd rather be here
than anywhere...

As I left
I thought things will change,
but everyday just feels the same
on that runaway train...

Once, we were just two lost souls
breathing in stereo
to the rythm of the waves,
as we were about to become one...

SUMMER

Exist a little less.
Live a little more.
Take a little risk.
Start to explore.
Open your heart.
Reveal you core.
Exist a little less.
Live a little more!

Wander you do
'cause wander you must.
With a smile on your face
and shoes full of dust.
Wherever you go
just follow the sun.
With a mind wild & free
and a heart born to run.
May your spirits be high
wherever you roam.
Stay true to your soul,
keep rambling on.

Side by side,
half asleep,
your fingers on my back
never skip a beat.

Half asleep
face to face,
my heart beats
to your fingers' pace.

Side by side,
I realise,
half asleep,
music never dies...

On this Indian summer night
I roam the streets,
while the city sleeps.
And I'm passing by
the laundromat
where we once met,
as you brought the stories
and I brought the wine.

This feels right and I'm letting it,
what else do I need to know?
Please don't be afraid my love
I will never tire of you!

I hope this feels right and you're letting it,
we'll figure this out over time.
I'll never tire of yours my love,
I hope you'll never tire of mine.

I drove like a maniac.
From the dykes of the Netherlands
to the shores of Normandy.
I drove to the end of Europe
only to forget you,
lose every memory of you.

And yet,
I only lost myself...

My heart, it skipped a beat
on this wildest of nights,
as your lips touched mine
under neon lights.

I whispered I love you,
you stepped back and smiled.
"I'm drunk..." you said
as you left me behind...

You're the paper,
you're the pen,
you're all the inbetween.

You're the poem,
you're the art,
you're the ember of my heart...

Poets are fools
so they say.
Though I enjoy the foolery.

For poets are,
no less is true,
really only fools for you...

In a world full of turmoil
women are the fiercest fighters there are.

Why?

They simply always had to be!

SUMMER

Every sunset reminds me
of the beach in Normandy.

Where you sipped wine
out of a paper cup.
Watching the sun
dive into the blue sea.

While you wore my hoodie
and I loved it....

People hated you
but to me you've always been cool.
With your punk shirts,
back in high School.

Lately you've been on my mind
cause to me you've always been kind.
Especially that one summer night
I'm still not quite sure why.

Now I feel like a fool
because to me you've always been cool.
But I never told you
back in high School...

Here I am,
decades later,
and I still have to smile
when I think abou you...

Your ability
to read me like a book
is both,
terrifying
and utterly beautiful...

Different cities,
different coasts,
an ocean apart,
and yet so close,
as two hearts
become one soul...

I've been so many places,
have seen so many faces,
and yet,
yours is the one I dream of
every night...

SUMMER

I still think
of those summer days
when we met in Paris.

But those days are past now
where they must remain
for I won't ever see you again...

I feel so wild
when I'm with you.
And when you leave
I feel oh so blue...

I'm just another boy.
Certainly not one of a kind.
But you made me feel special
all of the time...

AUTUMN

AUTUMN

Summer fades to autumn shades,
the cold pierces my summer skin.
Mist turned into velvet shapes
by daylight's virgin gleam.

And here I stand in solitude,
but don't you worry about me.
For I just wait, like lovers do
patient for her company.

Just like summer
you stole my heart
and slipped away
with the autumn winds...

Oh, I feel lost
in space and time.
Caught up
in the weirdness of my mind.

And if I leave,
I feel left behind.
And if I stay,
I feel trapped inside.

That's the way it is
for the strange and the kind –
dazed and confused
all of the time.

You loved me as a poet.
I loved you as you were.
But you demanded to be poetry
while all you've ever been was words...

I hope that you're happy,
and I hope that you smile,
and I hope that for once
you don't have to cry.

And I hope that you make it,
and I hope you're not sore.
But most of all I hope
that you're happier than before.

Completely out of breath I sit on the tram I just caught, because – yet again – I allowed myself too much time this morning.

Hmm, time... What's the point of time anyway? This invisible force that drives us nonstop and won't even let us wait 5 minutes for the next tram. We call it precious and yet we let it dominate our lives mercilessly. We set deadlines, appointments, clock our days as efficiently as possible – after all, "Dont't waste your time" is the motto, isn't it?

Oh, what pathetic fools we are...

We don't waste time – we just waste our lives!

Adults are like,
this... mess.
Existing too much,
living too less.

Their lives are so dull –
everything's grey and plain.
While all they just want
is to see colors again.

I know it is hard,
but I promise it helps:
go get some paint,
add color yourselves.

I don't get it...
Where's your reward in that?!

Honey,
I don't run on rewards...

I miss the times
we knew nothing
and imagined everything...

The day you cheated at Mario Kart
I should have known
that cheating
is part of your game...

This poem is everything
you want it to be...

Whenever I hear that old song play
it hits my body in different ways.
It picks me up, takes me away.
Say, can you still relate?

Maybe this is our fate.
We learned a lot in difficult ways.
Say, do you still remember these days?
I do, when that old song plays...

I have to leave
eventhough
I can't hide
what I'm running from,
that much I know.
But I can never come back
if I don't go...

Why are you so sad all the time?

Well,
there's just no use in a happy poet,
my dear...

You always screamed the loudest,
when you've been silent...

Our souls are like magnets
I suppose...
If we feel different
we're drawn together,
and if we fell the same
we push us apart

I wander about
the unbeaten paths of life,
alone most of the time.
Some cross my path
along the way,
yet none dare to stay.
For they know I won't let them...

I tried so hard
to change the world
while all it did
was changing me...

You're running from the past
with a heavy heart and a troubled mind.
But honey, don't you get it?
It's impossible to outrun time...

I'm sorry,
for invading your space.
For trying to be the key
while I've been the cage...

I know it is hopeless,
at least so it seems.
But the lonliest poets
can only dare dream...

You know I can
sleep without you.
Oh, I can
breathe without you.
Spend all day
not thinking about you.
Oh you know
I can't...

Sometimes,
I want to be a poem you love...
But you don't care much,
about poetry as such...
Don't you?

They keep asking questions
but I've long stopped to reply.
They say it's easy,
but they don't realise
for me it is already
as heavy as can be.

Life overwhelms me
while they tell me „Stop to cry".
But I need to be Superman
to push the sun back in my sky.
This should be easy
but for me it is already
as heavy as can be.

I'd write you a poem
if you'd read the words.
I'd sing you a song
if I knew it'd be heard.
I'd write 1000 letters
only to plea.
Please love me
or hate me.
Just don't be indifferent to me...

What hurts the most
is the fact
that you will forget,
but I won't...

OH all my faith seems to be gone.
I'm saddened by **HUMANITY**.
WHAT the hell have we become?
WILL we ever regain dignity?
For hate is all **YOU** seem to tend.
When really, love is all you'd **MAKE**.
I'm sick **OF** it, we've reached the end!
My heart, **IT** is about to break...

NOTHING will ever change it seems.
I'M angry and confused.
AFRAID of all your violent screams!

EVERYTHING is up to us.
I put my dwindling faith in you.
'Cause **HOPE** is what I'ver never lost.

You don't know how it feels
when you're haunted
by the demons of your mind.

That if you run,
they'll stay close behind.
And if you stay,
they'll fuck with your mind.
But you think, you'll figure it out
in some time.
But you're left in the dark
all your life.

Oh, I do know
how it feels
when they try.

They feast on my fears
everyday... for the rest of my life.
And I fought for the change
that never came,
the more I tried.
But I think I figured it out
by this time.
When it's dark and you're lost,
your shadow gives you light.

Maybe, just maybe,
I loved you to death,
because I couldn't love myself
to save my life.

You see, loneliness is a dangerous thing. It slowly creeps up on you and at first you embrace it, you desire this bitter sweet melancholy it brings. It's like a drug and just like any other drug, it fucks your mind and before you know it, you're addicted to it....

Home is
where the heart is.
Say, is this why
I feel so homeless?

For home is
where I'll be
and home is
where I'm oh so lonely.

Cause my mind
roams here and there,
while my heart
is always elsewhere...

Why is the world
in such a terrible state?
Why do so many people
only love to hate?
Why can't we help others
when we see them fall?
Why are our minds
so god damn small?

Sometimes...
I feel like a sheep
in a world full of wolves...

My head is a room
I can't get out of.
Walls, I can't get through....

I tried to drown
my memories of you,
but those bastards are
pretty good swimmers...

Sometimes
being around people
makes me feel the lonliest...

You've got to go, I got to know,
just like all the seasons do.
Eventually you told me so,
eventually I should have known...

I wish I could stay forever,
but I've got to catch a bus...

Exist a little less
live a little more.
Take a little risk
start to explore.
Open your heart
reveal your core.
Exist a little less
live a little more...

— poet on a bus

@poetonabus

Life is wondrous sometimes. Two kindred souls, lonely on their paths through the endless universe – side by side, almost parallel, yet not quite. Visiting the same places, meeting each other without knowing the other exists. And yet they have to wait almost half a lifetime to find each other on that fateful evening in January.

Surely a cruel game of fate, it seems. Or might it be different? Couldn't it be that fate was just waiting for this one moment to bring the two together – the right place, the right time? Yes, that's how it must have been.

Well, it came as it had to, as their paths crossed and as the souls finally touched, in those last hours of January, a jolt went through time and space. A storm of emotions - every single one a person is able to feel ,flowed through the two souls. Joy, sadness, guilt, warmth, all surrounded by nothing but love. A love so pure as neither of them ever knew...

Well... I guess that's how it is when a new world is born...

To whom it may concern:
your soul is beautiful!